What Happens at the Zoo

by Arthur Shay

REILLY & LEE BOOKS • CHICAGO

This book is for the late Jim Hurlbut of NBC, who worked for years on "Zoo Parade" to teach children the wonder of animals.

For their patient help, the author would like to thank the staffs of the Chicago area's Lincoln Park and Brookfield Zoos; the San Diego Zoo; the St. Louis Zoo; the Jacksonville, Florida, Zoo; the Little Rock, Arkansas, Zoo; the Central Park Zoo, New York City; and Willie de Beer, animal catcher. Thanks are also due to NBC, *Sports Illustrated*, and *Life* magazine for permission to use pictures shot on assignment for them. Polar-bear-feeding picture by Dick Shay.

Published by Reilly & Lee Books, a division of Henry Regnery Company
114 West Illinois Street, Chicago, Illinois 60610
Manufactured in the United States of America
Library of Congress Catalog Card Number: 71–143868

To Parents and Teachers

The bonnet monkey is a small, lovable primate whose head and body can easily fit through the bars of its cage until it is a year old. At that age it must decide whether to live outside, in the spacious greenery of the zoo, or inside the cage, which is not so green, but where the social security is top rate. Caged monkeys have free food, protection from natural enemies, shelter, and medical care—as well as funny people to look at when things get boring.

Not surprisingly, no bonnet monkey—at least at Brookfield Zoo, near Chicago—has yet opted for the outside.

When zoo keepers get together, they often discuss the relative advantages to the animals of zoo versus wild life. It is generally agreed that animals live longer and happier lives in captivity. Several animal psychologists affirm that the mental state of zoo animals is probably calmer than that of wild animals running free.

The psychologists' findings seem confirmed by the fact that most zoos have a serious encroachment problem. Wild birds, snakes, weasels, deer, skunks, raccoons—even pets—try to sneak into captivity to enjoy the soft life.

The encroachment problem is only one of many faced by zoo keepers. I hope that some of the pictures in this book will give my young readers a better idea of what happens behind the scenes at the zoo, and will spur discussions, ranging from Africa to your nearest zoo, among parents, teachers, and young people.

Arthur Shay

Many cities have their own zoos, where you can see all sorts of animals, birds, and reptiles. Zoo keepers get their animals from dealers or from other zoos all over the world. The dealers buy the animals from animal catchers, such as this member of a giraffe-capturing team in Tanzania, Africa.

Zoo managers try to think of new ways to interest people in coming to the zoo. Here a man puts up a billboard in the city, inviting the public to come to the zoo. Some of the larger zoos have sightseeing buses to make it easier for their visitors to get around in the zoo itself.

Zoo managers want their younger guests to enjoy themselves.

Certain zoos have special events—such as this quarter-mile tortoise race, which takes three hours to run!

The St. Louis Zoo has a full
schedule of animal shows
to entertain its guests.
The chimpanzees ride
ponies as well as bikes.
The elephants in this zoo
"barber shop" can also
play volleyball, dance,
and swing a bat.

Brookfield Zoo, near
Chicago, has its own
performers: porpoises.
They leap over hurdles as
high as fifteen feet and
even shoot baskets!
Porpoises are friendly,
intelligent mammals, who
can actually "speak" to
other porpoises
underwater.

Each zoo animal has its own personality. This lion is so lazy—and its tongue is so tough—that it doesn't even bother to flick away the flies!

This Barbary sheep, on the other hand, is very active and likes to jump from rock to rock.

Zoo keepers try to provide homes for their animals like the ones the animals would have if they were living in the wilds. At Chicago's Lincoln Park Zoo, welders complete high steel foundations for cement walls that will seem like the side of a mountain and will become a home for mountain lions.

At the San Diego Zoo, a lucky mouse family gets a new loaf of bread to live in whenever they eat themselves out of house and home.

Nature protects many animals by making their skin color the same as the area they live in. Can you find the sea lion sunning himself among the artificial rocks?

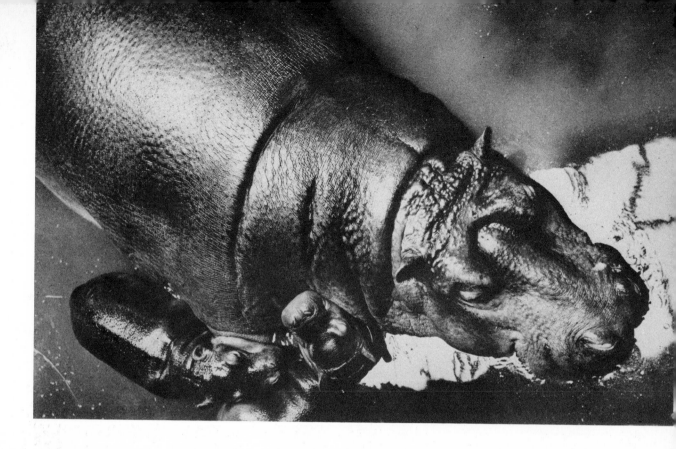

Thousands of gallons of water are used at the zoo each day. The animals like their water holes freshly filled. The mother hippo has to teach her twins to swim. The walrus likes to dive deeply and then pop his head up. Turtles like to take deep breaths and then stay underwater as long as they can.

The tiger enjoys his
garden-hose shower, but
this elephant has to be
coaxed into taking a bath!

Feeding the animals is a big job, and the zoo has several kitchens for preparing meals.

Horse meat is the favorite food of the meat eaters. The zoo keepers put vitamin pills in the meat and in some of the vegetables that go to the animals that don't eat meat. When the food is ready, attendants carry it from the kitchens to the hungry animals.

No matter how good a meal the "chef" prepares, or how much he serves, there are always some animals who want a little more.

The food at the zoo is so good that many non-zoo animals try to get some for themselves. It's easy for a chipmunk or a crow to outrun an elephant for a peanut. Squirrels and pigeons also like to visit the zoo. During migration seasons, stray birds usually land for a meal or two and sometimes stay to start new families.

Spiders spin their webs across the bars of the elephants' cage to catch insects attracted by the elephants.

Most animal mothers and fathers give their babies all the love and protection they need, just like human parents. Sometimes, however, a zoo baby is so delicate or weak that it needs help from the zoo keepers.

Modern zoo nurseries have the same kind of equipment that good hospitals have for human babies. The temperature in this special crib, called an "incubator," is exactly right for the baby that is sleeping in it.

A loving zoo attendant helps this baby gorilla get started toward the 500 pounds he will probably weigh when fully grown.

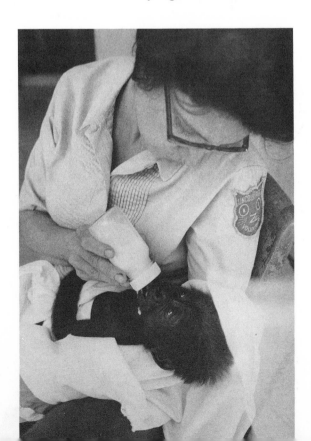

In the nursery, no one is allowed to handle the baby
animals but the attendants. Visitors to the children's
zoo, however, are encouraged to play with the young
animals. This is the place to stick out your tongue at a
snake [non-poisonous, of course], who does the same to
you. You can also hold the snake, if you're careful, and
study the old skins it has shed in its cage.

The temperature in this egg hatcher is at just the right level for hatching eggs. Snakes have a small egg tooth that helps them slit their way out of their eggs. Chicks peck their way out with their beaks.

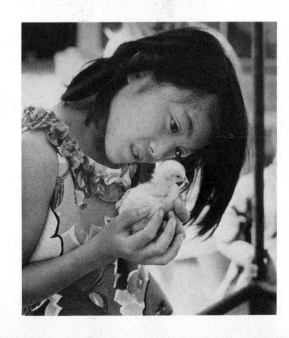

The zoo has its own hospital
for sick animals. This black
panther with a chest cold
makes a face even before
he gets his shot.

It takes two zoo keepers to
find a hedgehog's tummy for
a shot or to clip a raccoon's
toenails.

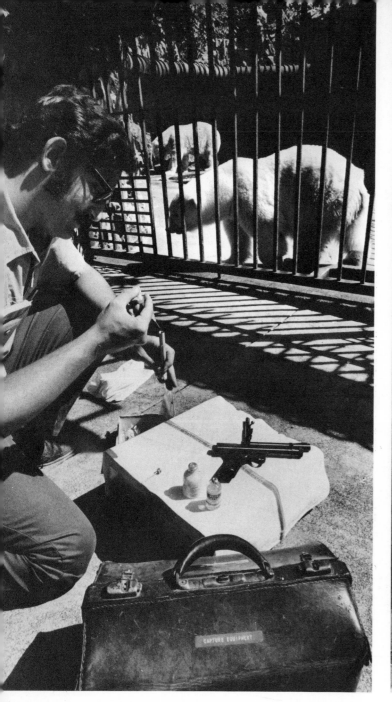

Mark Rosenthal studied animal health and behavior in college. Now he works as a "zoologist," helping to take care of the zoo's animals. Mark and the zoo's animal doctor, or "veterinarian," noticed that Ivan, a polar bear, seemed to have a toothache. So Mark took a gun from his "capture kit" and loaded it with a special dart containing a drug that can put a polar bear to sleep for several hours. Ivan didn't feel a thing when Mark fired the drug-dart into him.

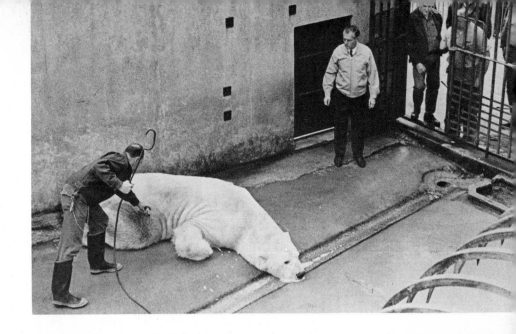

Soon Ivan fell asleep, and the zoo keepers helped the veterinarian pull out the bad tooth. To make sure that he wouldn't leave any painful bits of tooth in Ivan's gum, the doctor brought in a portable X-ray machine from the zoo hospital and X-rayed his patient right in the cage. Everything was fine.

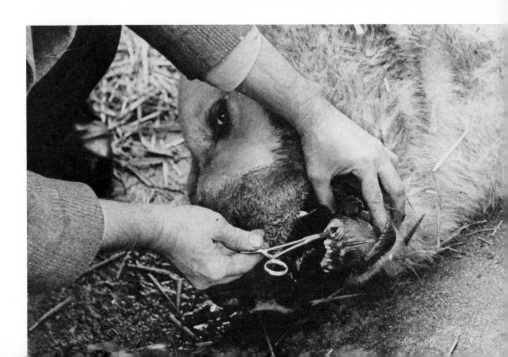

There's always something exciting happening at the zoo. One day each fall, the Brookfield Zoo's keepers go to the "monkey island" with brooms, sticks, nets, and cages. Their difficult job is to move the baboons, who live with the

mountain sheep, indoors for the winter so they won't freeze in Chicago's cold. The keepers use the sticks for chasing — not hitting! — and the nets for catching the baboons.

Each year the fastest and smartest baboon manages to avoid capture for several hours after all his friends have been moved to the warm monkey house. This ability to escape danger is very important to all animals living in the wild.

As we have seen, the men and women who work at the zoo do all they can to make zoos pleasant homes for the animals and nice places for people to visit. To keep things running smoothly, a few simple rules are necessary—not for the animals, who are usually well-behaved, but for the *people*.

When *you* visit a zoo, you should obey the signs — and please remember that you look just as funny to the animals as they do to you!